EASY PIANO

LEONARD COHEN

Cover photo: Getty Images / Michael Putland

ISBN 978-1-5400-0230-3

7777 W. BLUEMOUND RD. P.O. BOX 13819 MILWAUKEE, WI 53213

In Australia Contact:
Hal Leonard Australia Pty. Ltd.
4 Lentara Court
Cheltenham, Victoria, 3192 Australia
Email: ausadmin@halleonard.com.au

Visit Hal Leonard Online at
www.halleonard.com

DANCE ME TO
THE END OF LOVE

Words and Music by
LEONARD COHEN

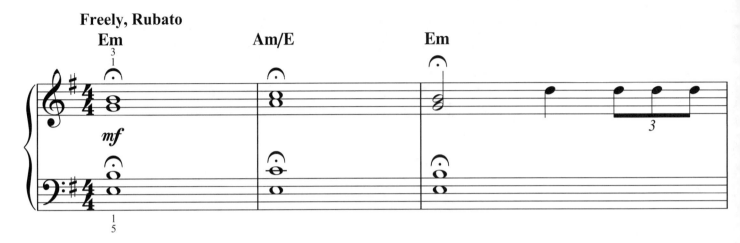

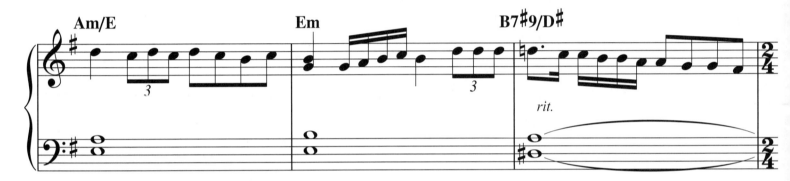

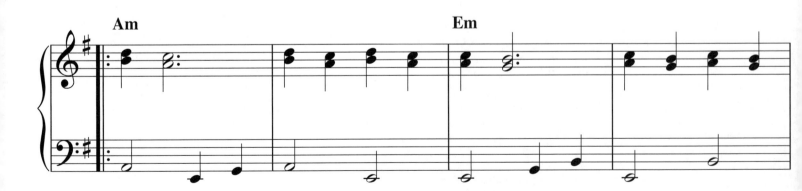

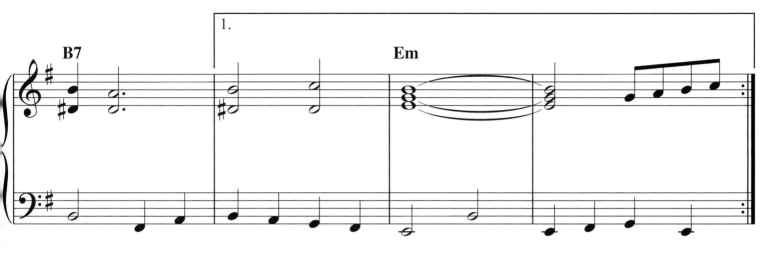

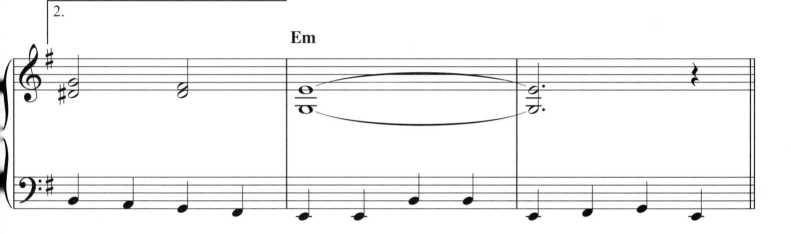

Dance me ___ to your beau - ty ___ with a burn - ing vi - o - lin. __
Dance me ___ to the wed - ding ___ now, __ dance me on and on. __
Dance me ___ to your beau - ty ___ with a burn - ing vi - o - lin. __

Dance me through the pan - ic ___ till I'm
Dance me ver - y ten - der - ly and dance __
Dance me through the pan - ic ___ till I'm

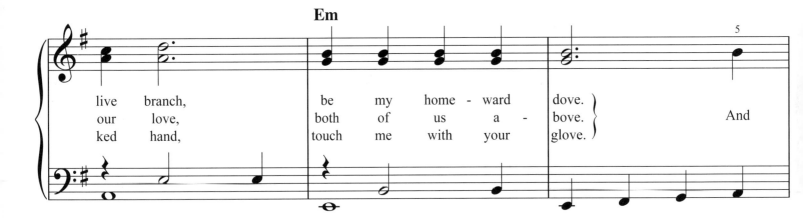

Em   Am

love.   Let   me   see   your
                                 Dance me   to   the

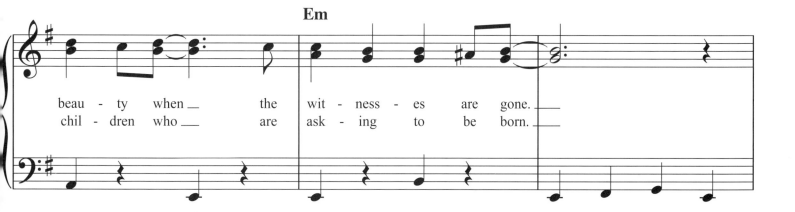

                                      Em

beau - ty when __   the wit - ness - es are gone. __
chil - dren who __   are ask - ing to   be   born. __

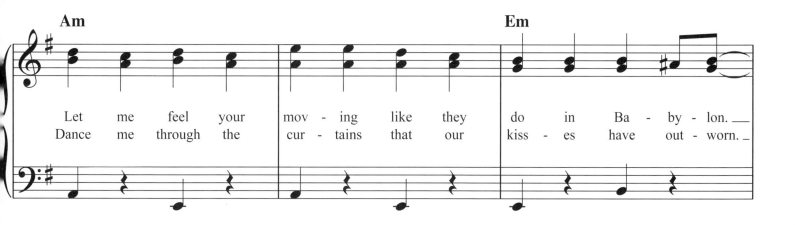

Am   Em

Let   me   feel   your   mov - ing like they   do   in   Ba - by - lon. __
Dance me   through the   cur - tains that our   kiss - es have out - worn. __

Am

__   Show me   slow - ly   what I   on - ly
__   Raise a   tent   of   shel - ter now, though

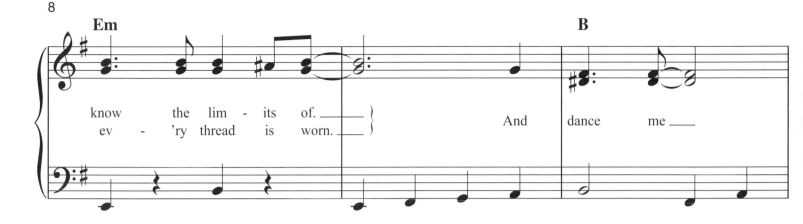

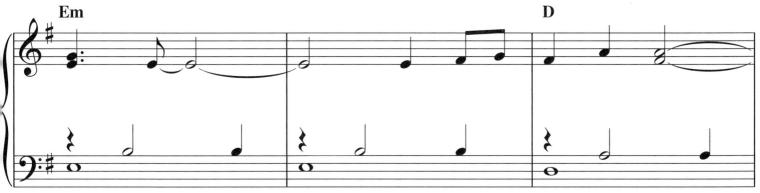

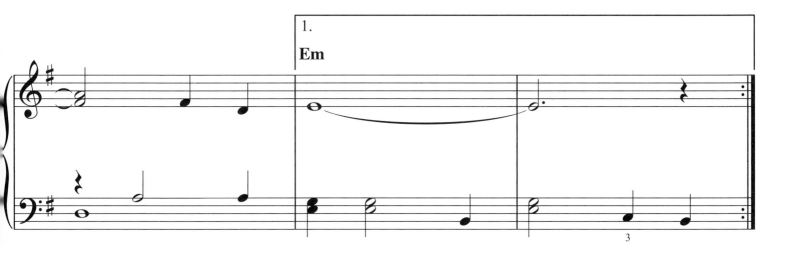

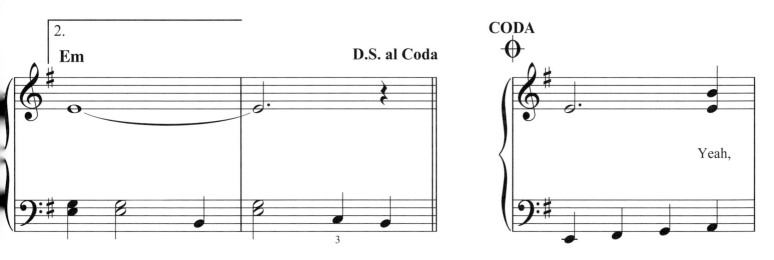

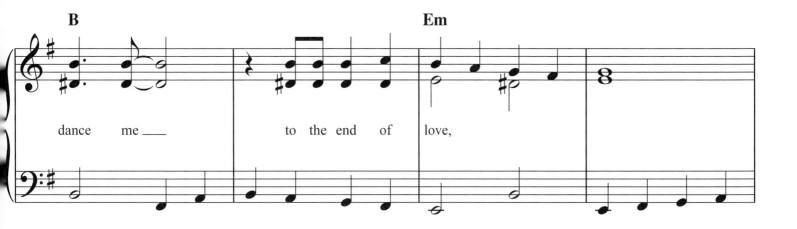

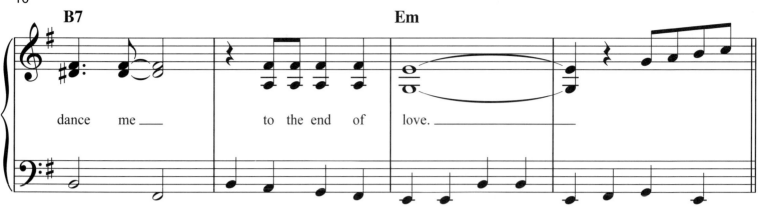

dance me ___ to the end of love. ___

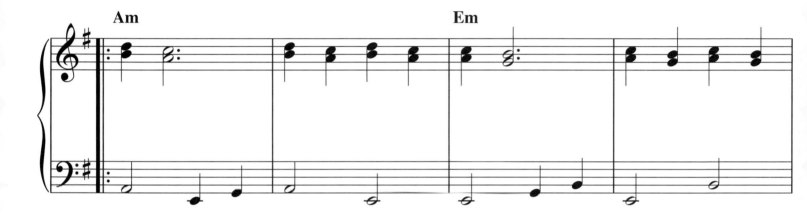

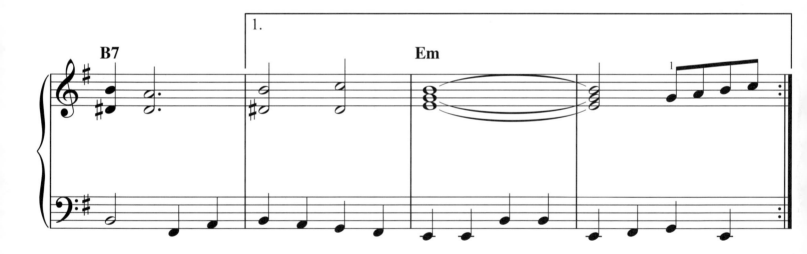

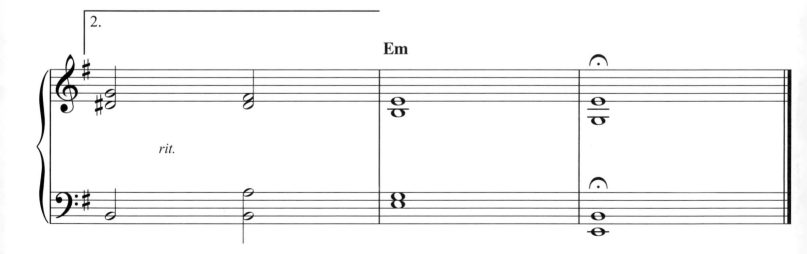

BIRD ON THE WIRE
(Bird on a Wire)

Words and Music by
LEONARD COHEN

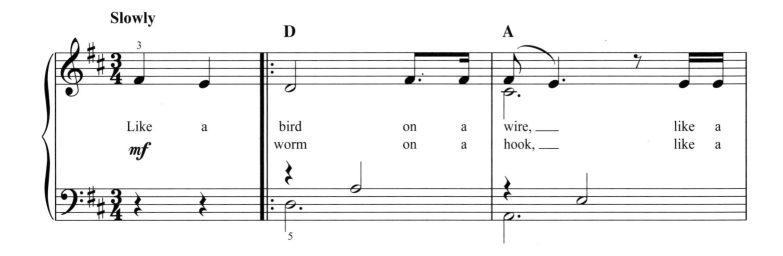

Like a bird on a wire, _____ like a
worm on a hook, _____ like a

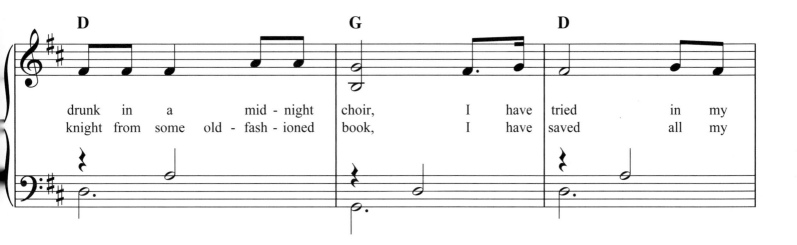

drunk in a mid-night choir, I have tried in my
knight from some old-fash-ioned book, I have saved in all my

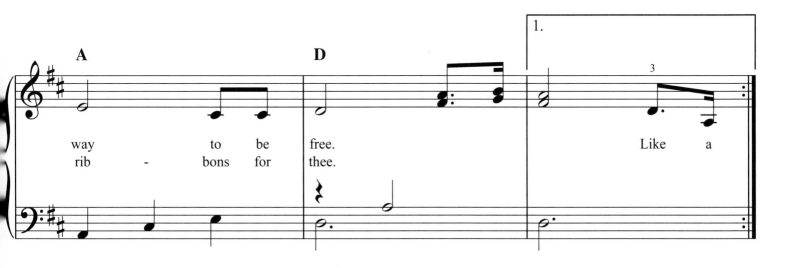

way to be free.
rib-bons for thee.

Like a

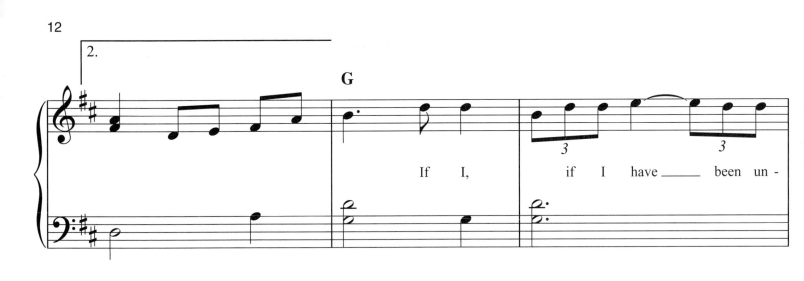

2.

G

If I, if I have _____ been un-

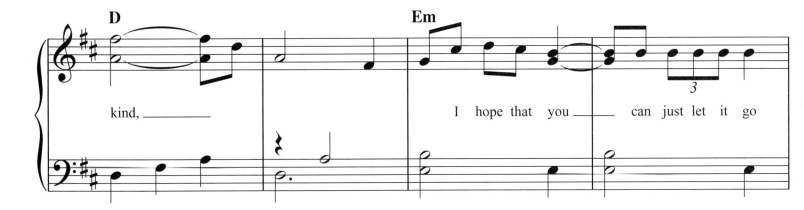

D

Em

kind, _____ I hope that you ___ can just let it go

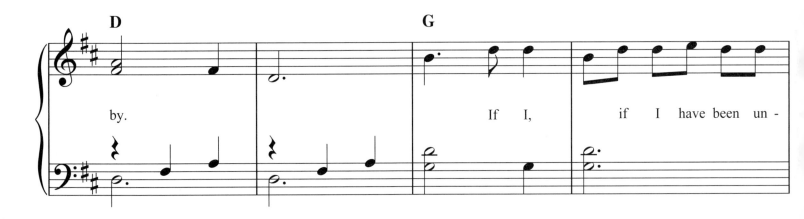

D

G

by. If I, if I have been un-

D

Em

true, _____ I hope you know ___ it was nev - er for

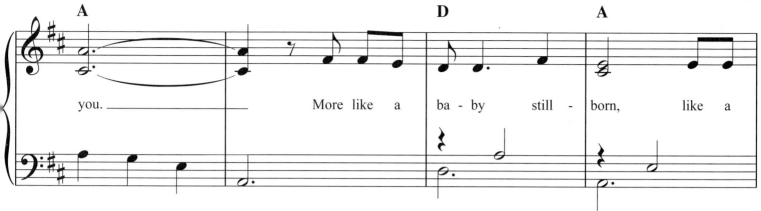

you. _____ More like a ba - by still - born, like a

beast with his horn, I have torn ev - 'ry -

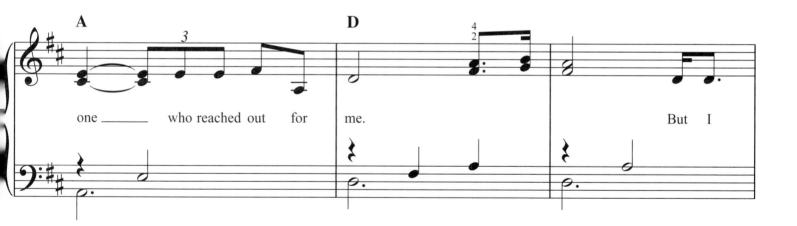

one _____ who reached out for me. But I

swear by this song, and by all that I have done wrong,

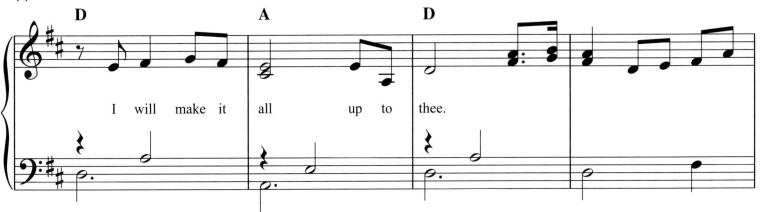

I will make it all up to thee.

I saw a beg - gar lean - ing on his wood - en crutch. ____

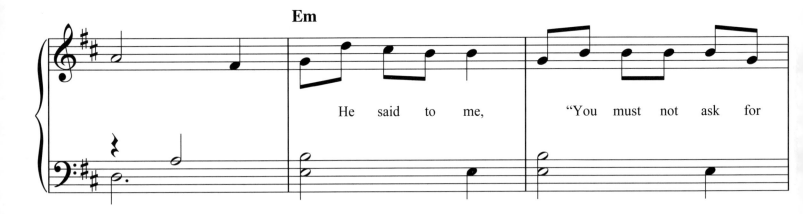

He said to me, "You must not ask for

so much." ____ And a pret - ty wom - an

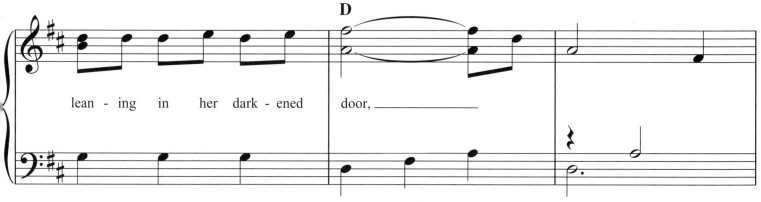

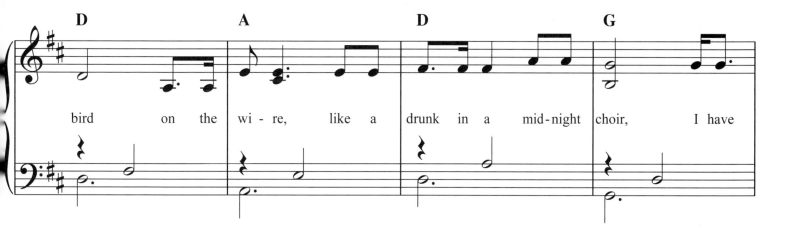

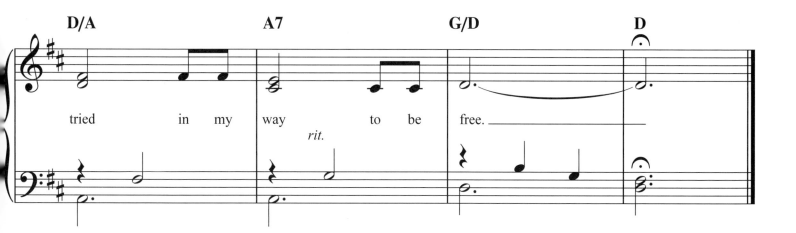

EVERYBODY KNOWS

Words and Music by LEONARD COHEN
and SHARON ROBINSON

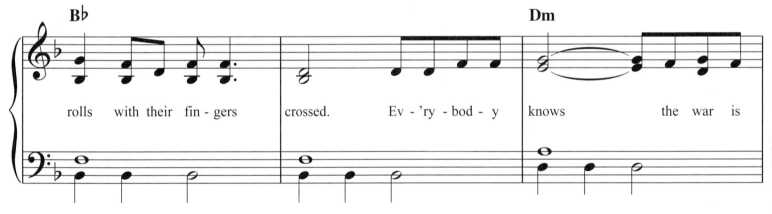

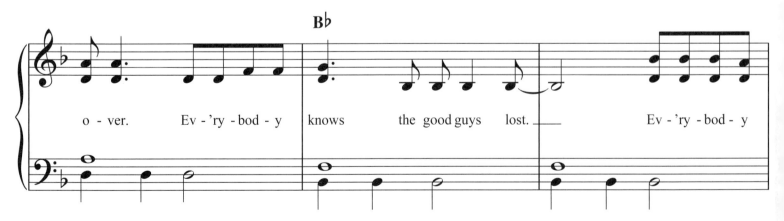

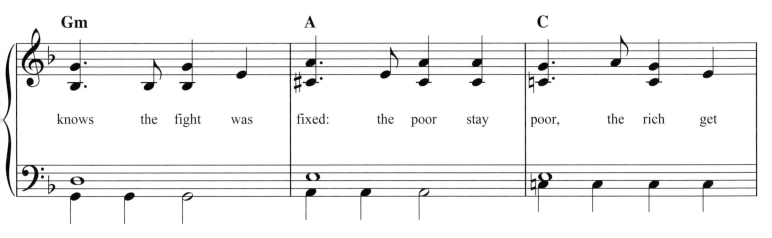

knows the fight was fixed: the poor stay poor, the rich get

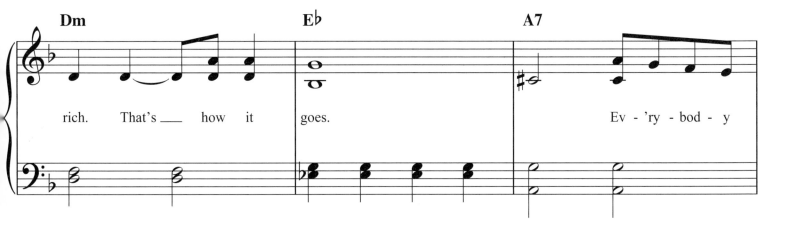

rich. That's ___ how it goes. Ev - 'ry - bod - y

knows. 2. Ev - 'ry - bod - y knows that the boat is

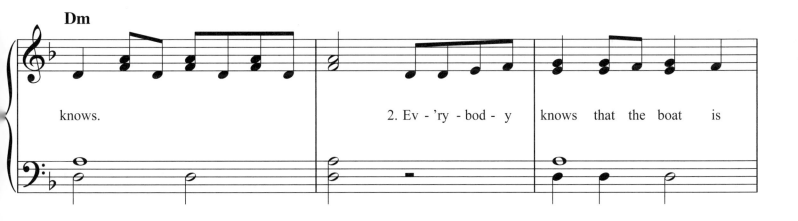

leak - ing. Ev - 'ry - bod - y knows the cap - tain lied. Ev - 'ry - bod - y

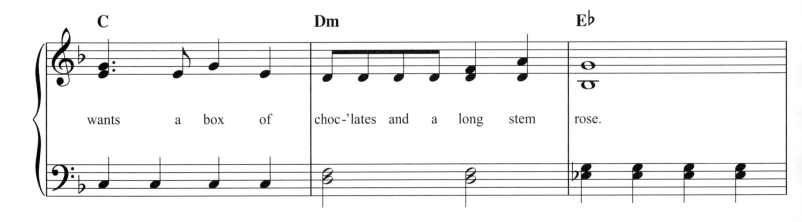

knows that you love me, ba - by. Ev - 'ry - bod - y knows that you real - ly do.

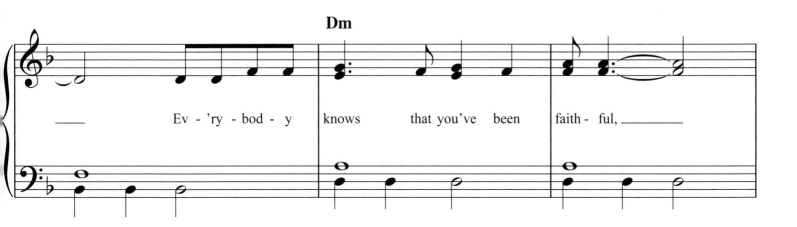

Ev - 'ry - bod - y knows that you've been faith - ful, _____

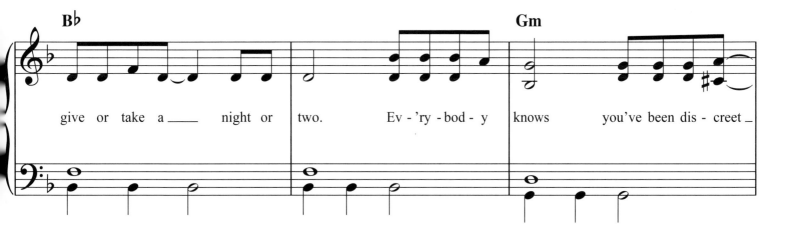

give or take a ___ night or two. Ev - 'ry - bod - y knows you've been dis - creet _

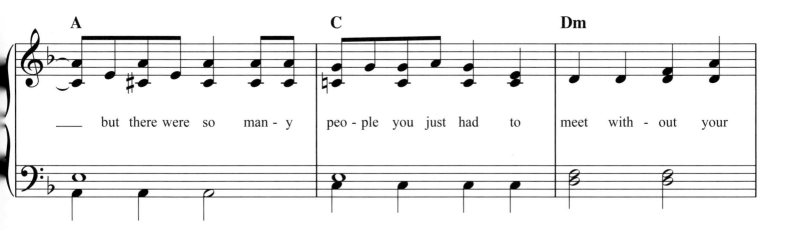

___ but there were so man - y peo - ple you just had to meet with - out your

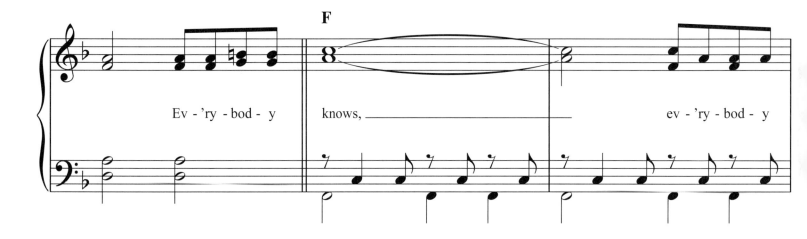

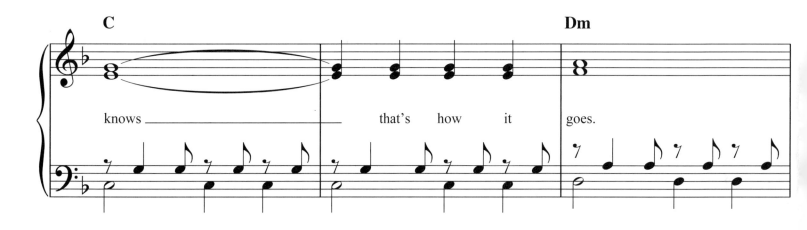

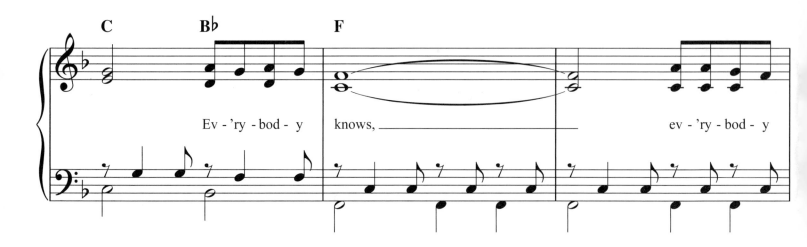

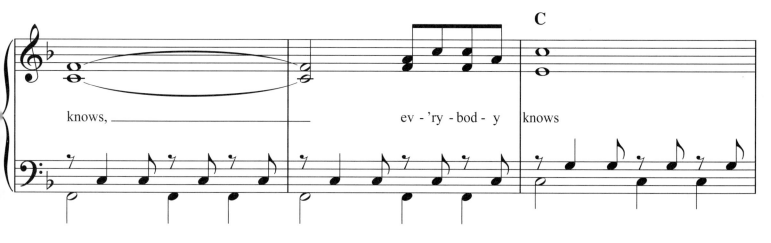

knows, _____ ev - 'ry - bod - y knows

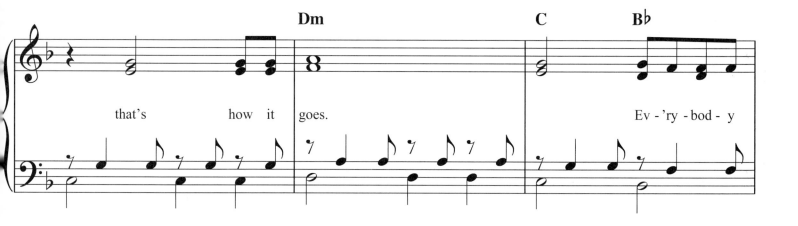

Dm that's how it goes. **C** **B♭** Ev - 'ry - bod - y

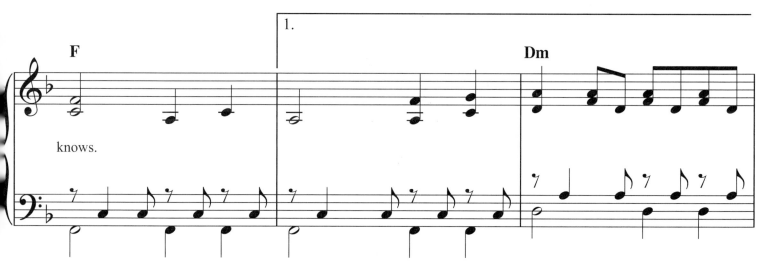

F knows. **Dm**

1.

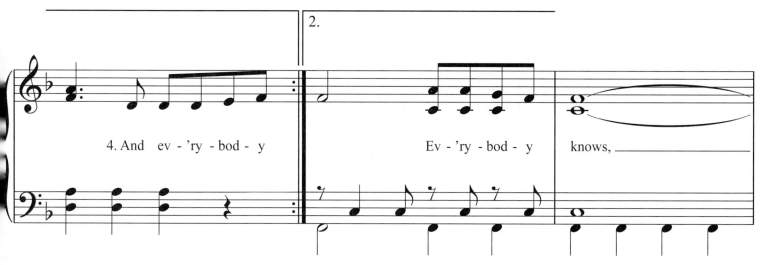

2.

4. And ev - 'ry - bod - y Ev - 'ry - bod - y knows, _____

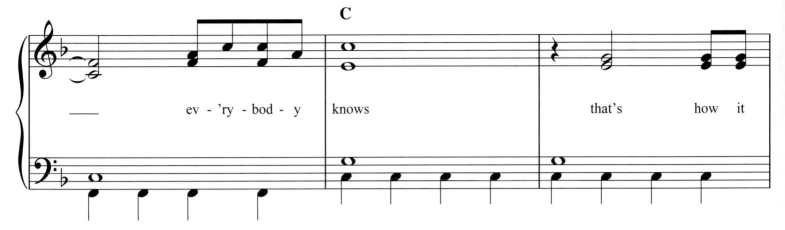

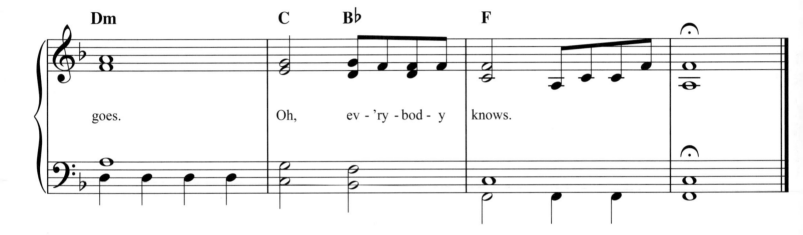

Additional Lyrics

4. And everybody knows that it's now or never.
   Everybody knows that it's me or you.
   And everybody knows that you live forever
   When you've done a line or two.
   Everybody knows the deal is rotten:
   Old Black Joe's still pickin' cotton
   For your ribbons and bows. And everybody knows.

5. Everybody knows that the plague is coming.
   Everybody knows that it's moving fast.
   Everybody knows that the naked man and woman
   Are just a shining artifact of the past.
   Everybody knows the scene is dead,
   But there's gonna be a meter on your bed
   That will disclose what everybody knows.

6. And everybody knows that you're in trouble.
   Everybody knows what you've been through,
   From the bloody cross on top of Calvary
   To the beach of Malibu.
   Everybody knows it's coming apart:
   Take one last look at this Sacred Heart
   Before it blows. And everybody knows.

FAMOUS BLUE RAINCOAT

Words and Music by
LEONARD COHEN

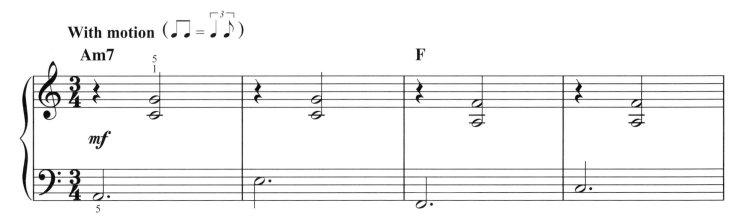

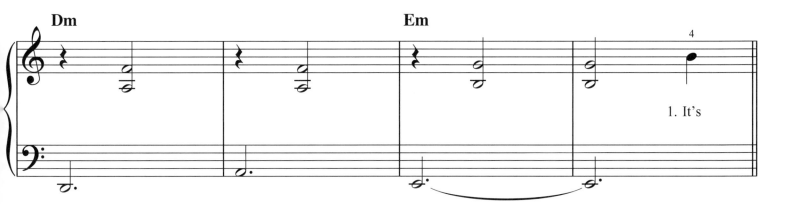

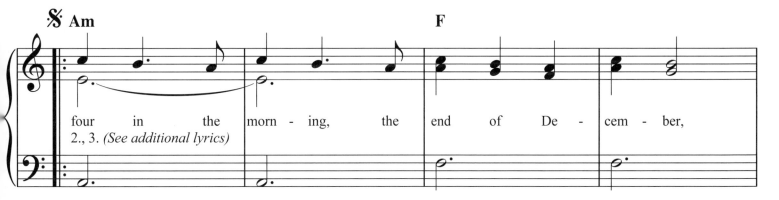

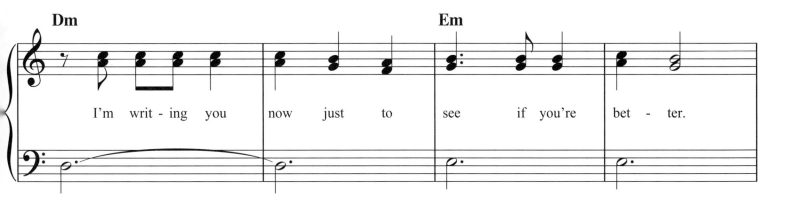

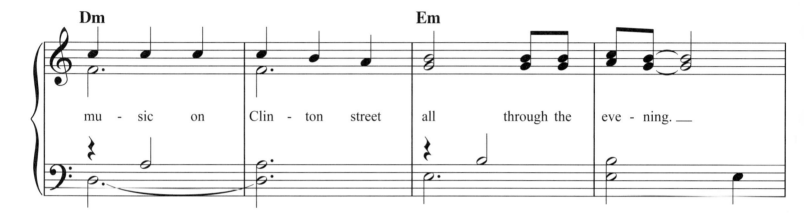

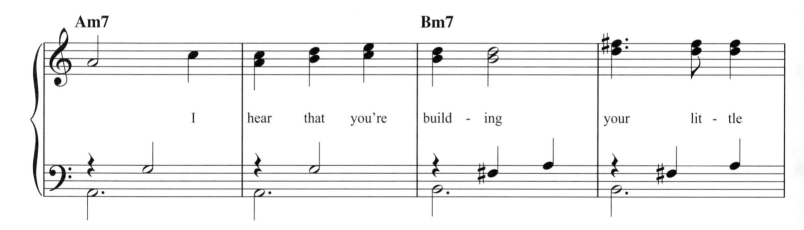

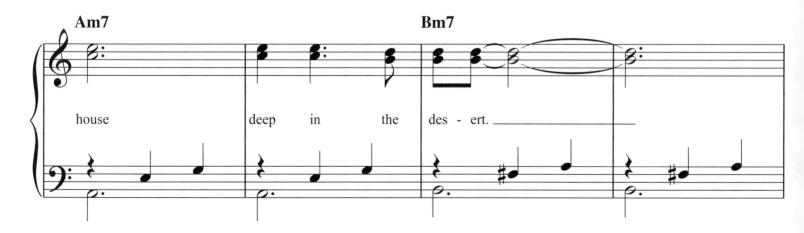

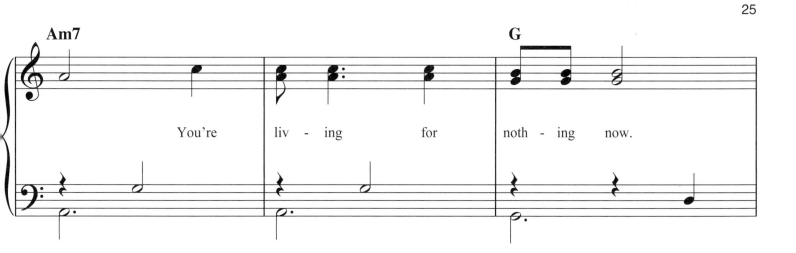

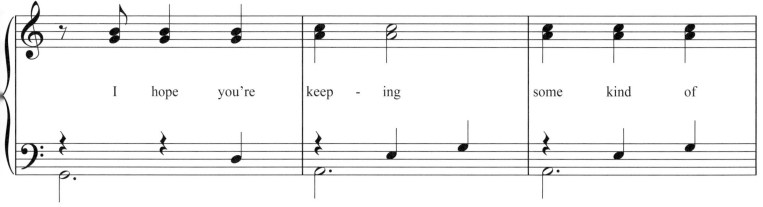

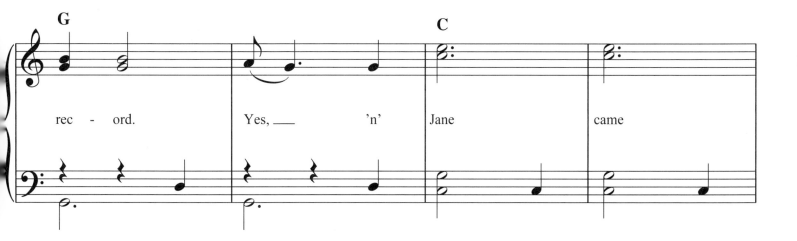

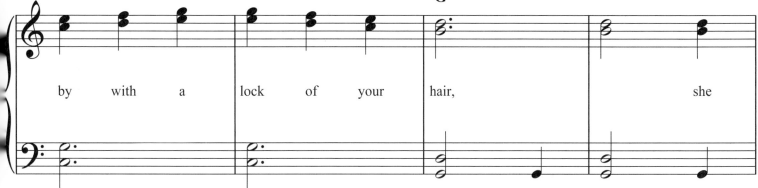

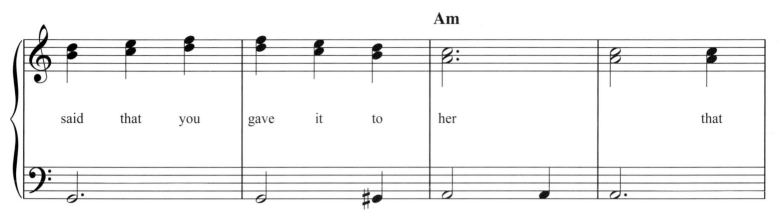

said that you gave it to her   that

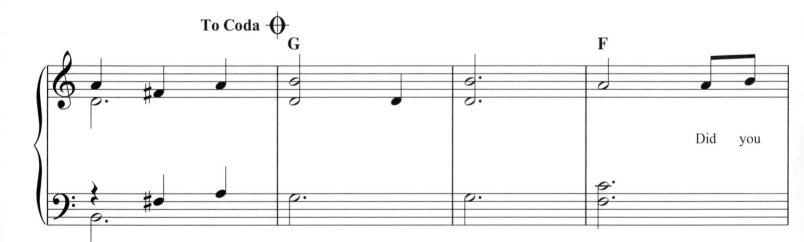

night that you planned to go clear.

Did you

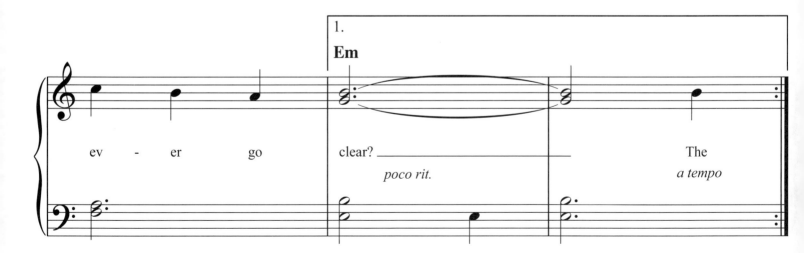

ev - er go clear?   The

poco rit.   *a tempo*

clear?

poco rit.

D.S. al Coda

CODA

G

And

a tempo

And

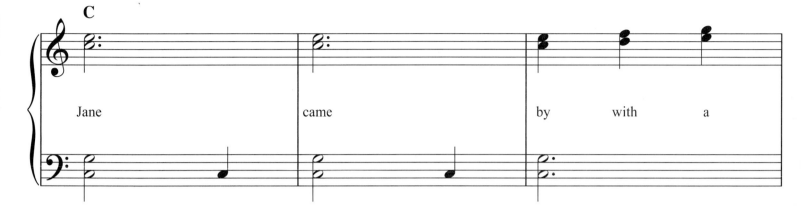

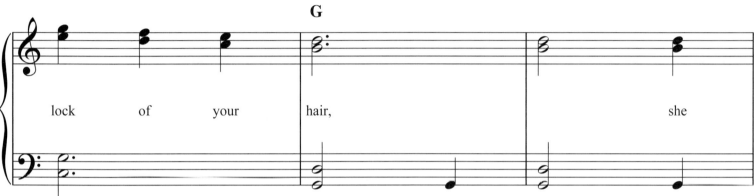

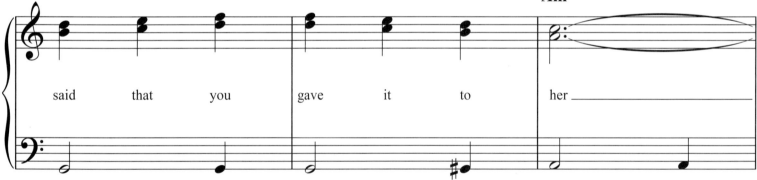

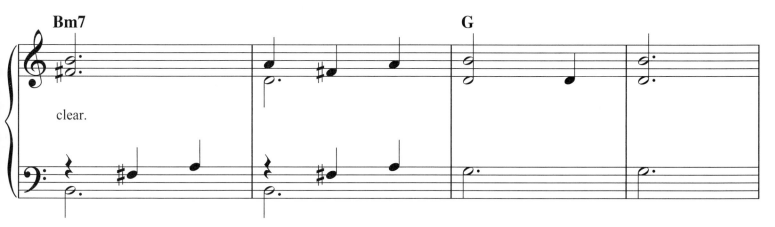

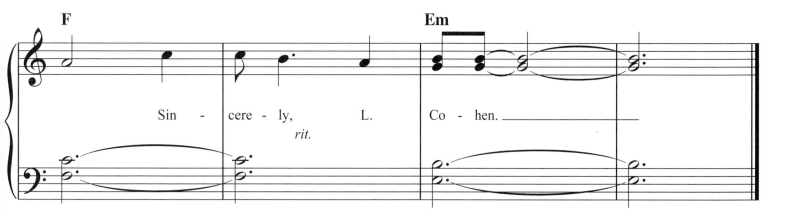

Additional Lyrics

2. The last time we saw you, you looked so much older
   Your famous blue raincoat was torn at the shoulder
   You'd been to the station to meet ev'ry train
   You came home with Lili Marlene
   And treated my woman to a flake of your life
   And when she came back she was nobody's wife.

   Well, I see you there with a rose in your teeth
   One more thin gypsy thief
   Well, I see Jane's away, she sends her regards.

3. And what can I tell my brother, my killer
   What can I possibly say?
   I guess that I miss you, I guess I forgive you
   I'm glad you stood in my way
   If you ever come by here for Jane or for me
   Well, your enemy is sleeping and his woman is free.

   Yes, thanks for the trouble you took from her eyes
   I thought it was there for good, so I never tried.

THE FUTURE

Words and Music by
LEONARD COHEN

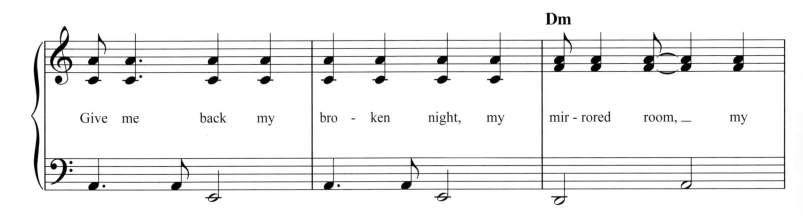

Give me back my broken night, my mir-rored room, — my

se - cret life, — it's lone - ly here, there's no one left to tor -

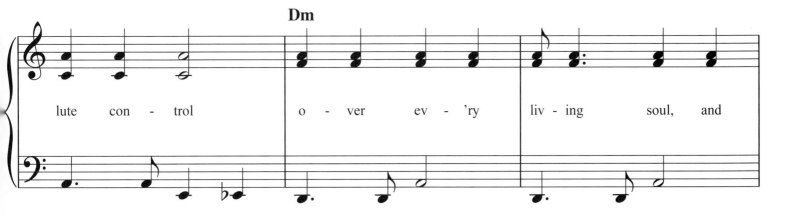

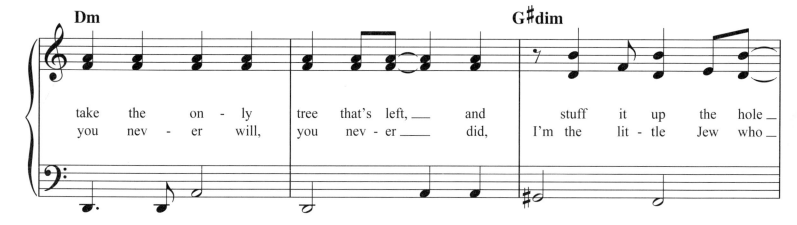

take the on - ly tree that's left, ___ and stuff it up the hole ___
you nev - er will, you nev - er ___ did, I'm the lit - tle Jew who ___

___ in your cul - ture. _____
___ wrote the Bi - ble. _____

Give me back the Ber - lin Wall, give me Sta - lin and ___
I've seen na - tions rise and fall, I've heard their sto - ries,

___ Saint Paul, ___ I've seen the fu - ture, broth - er: it is
heard them all, ___ but love's the on - ly ___ en - gine of sur -

murder. _____
vi - val. _____

Things are go - ing to slide, _

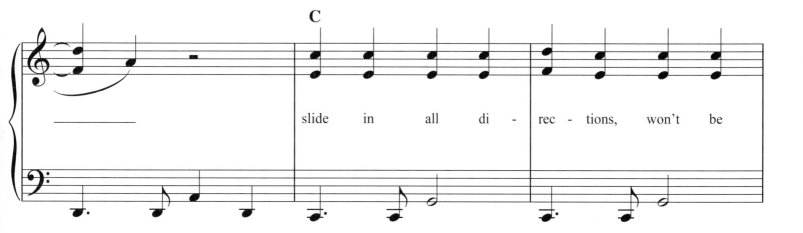

_____ slide in all di - rec - tions, won't be

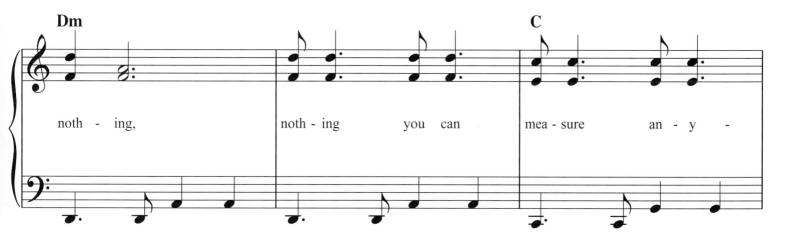

noth - ing, noth - ing you can mea - sure an - y -

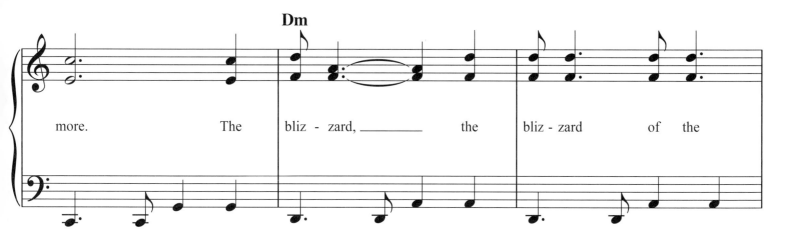

more. The bliz - zard, _____ the bliz - zard of the

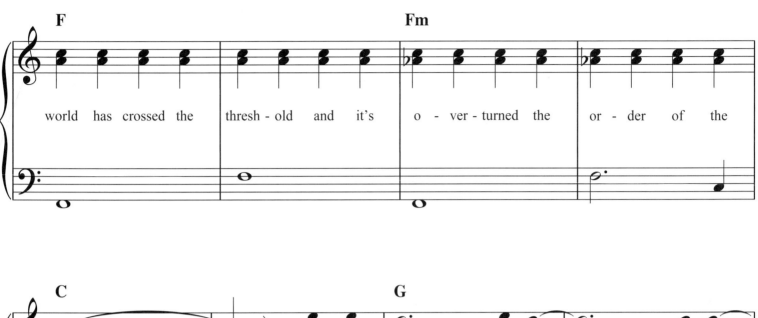

F   **Fm**

world has crossed the thresh - old and it's o - ver - turned the or - der of the

C   **G**

soul. _____ When they said, "Re - pent, ___ re - pent." _

Am   **To Coda** ⊕ | **1.**

— I won - der what they meant. _

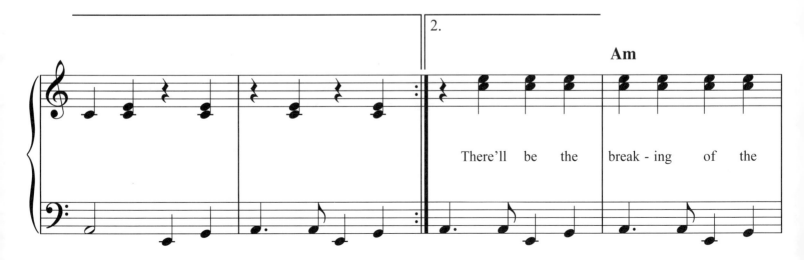

| **2.**

                                             Am

There'll be the break - ing of the

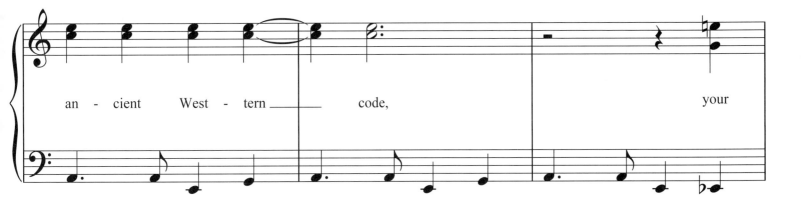

an - cient West - tern _____ code, your

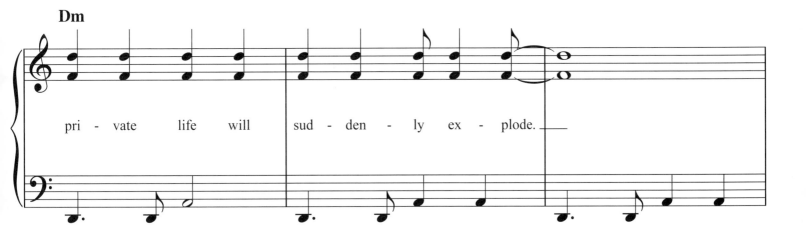

Dm

pri - vate life will sud - den - ly ex - plode. _____

Am

There'll be phan - toms, there'll be fires ___ on the road, and the

F7   **E7**

white man danc - ing.

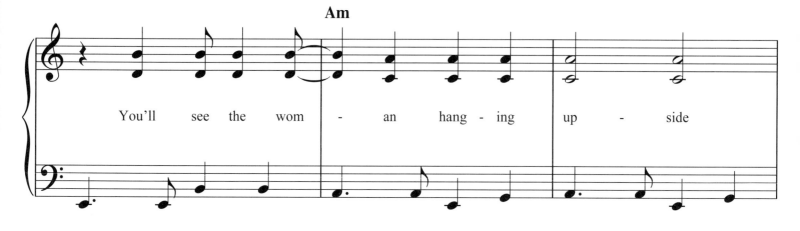

You'll see the wom - an hang - ing up - side

down, her fea - tures cov - ered

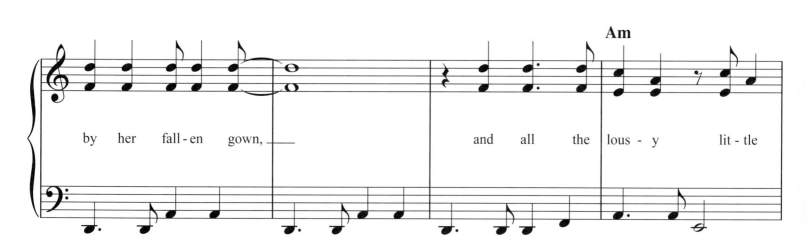

by her fall - en gown, and all the lous - y lit - tle

po - ets com - ing 'round, try - ing to sound like Char - lie Man - son,

E7

and the white man danc -

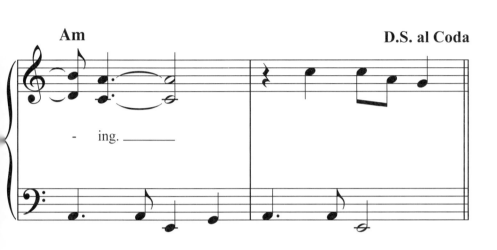

Am

D.S. al Coda

\- ing.

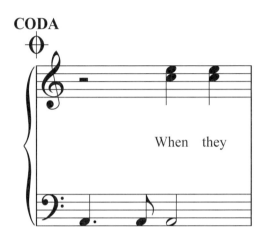

CODA

When they

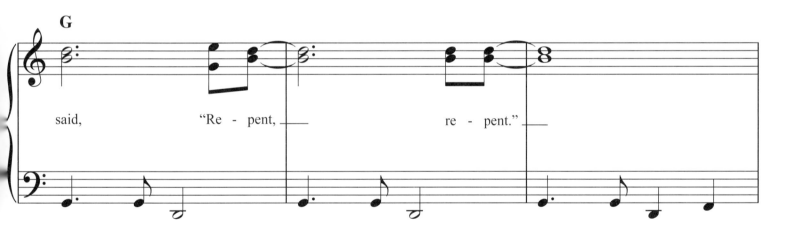

G

said, "Re - pent, re - pent."

Am

HALLELUJAH

Words and Music by
LEONARD COHEN

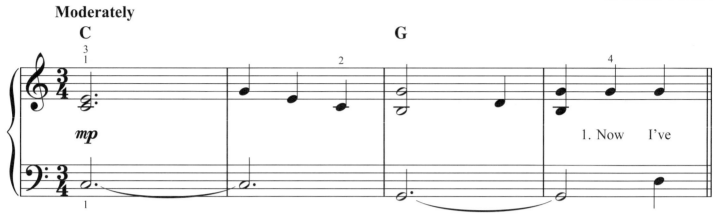

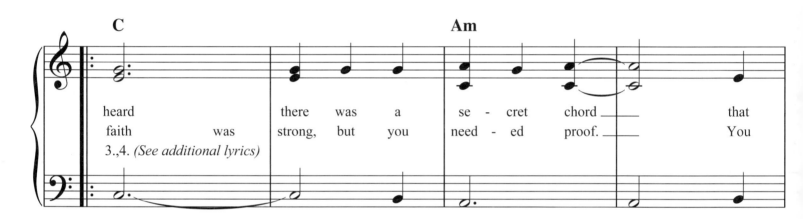

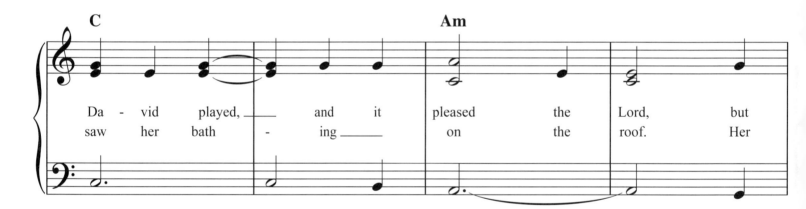

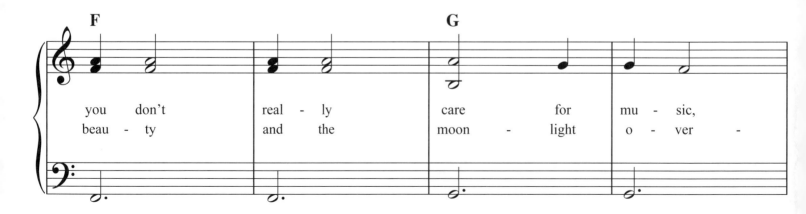

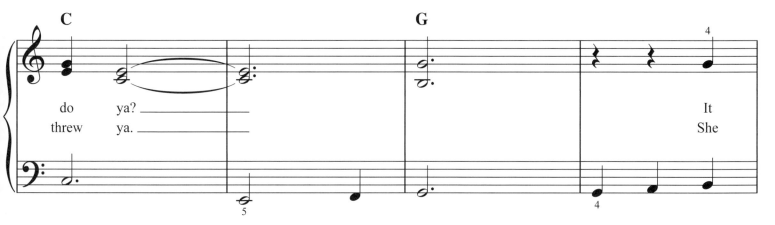

do ya? ____ ____ It
threw ya. ____ ____ She

goes like this: the fourth, the fifth, the
tied you to her kitch - en chair, she

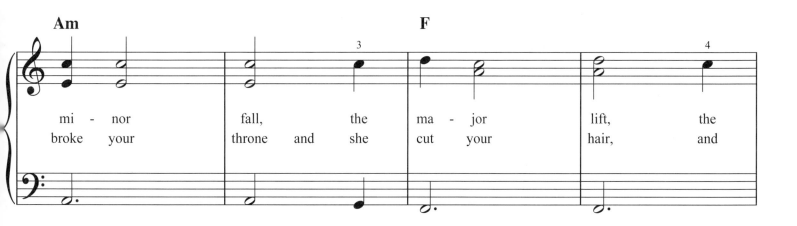

mi - nor fall, the ma - jor lift, the
broke your throne and she cut your hair, and

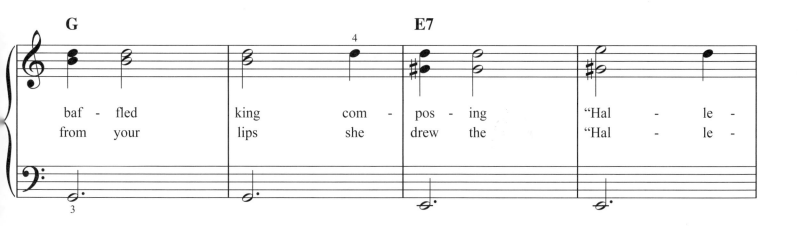

baf - fled king com - pos - ing "Hal - le -
from your lips she drew the "Hal - le -

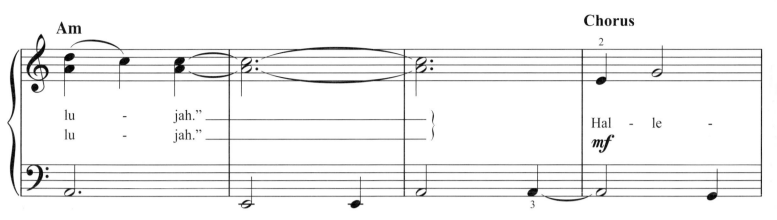

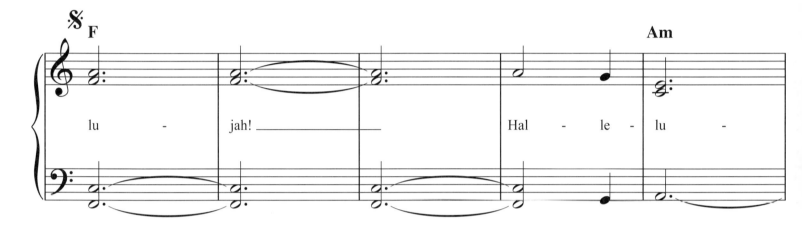

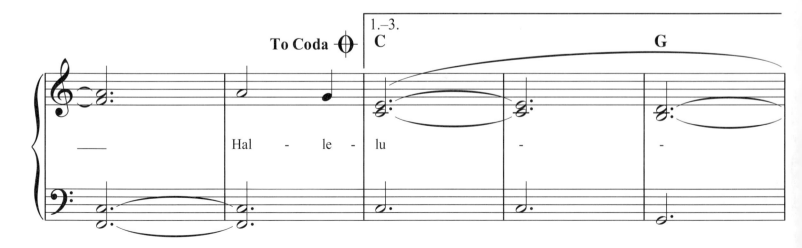

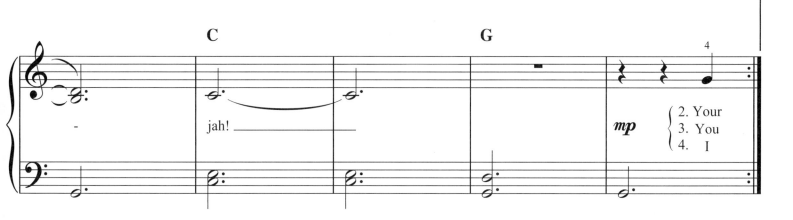

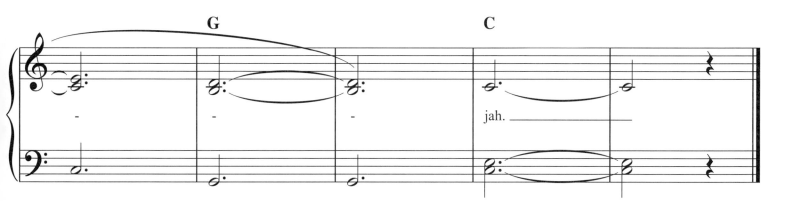

Additional Lyrics

3. You say I took the Name in vain:
I don't even know the Name,
But if I did, well, really, what's it to ya?
There's a blaze of light in every word.
It doesn't matter which are heard,
The holy or the broken Hallelujah.
Chorus

4. I did my best; it wasn't much.
I couldn't feel, so I tried to touch.
I've told the truth; I didn't come to fool ya.
And even though it all went wrong,
I'll stand before the Lord of Song
With nothing on my tongue but "Hallelujah."
Chorus

HEY, THAT'S NO WAY TO SAY GOODBYE

Words and Music by
LEONARD COHEN

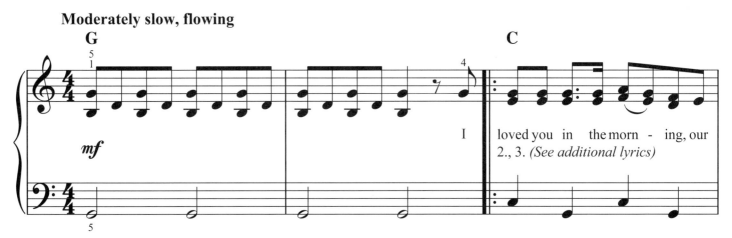

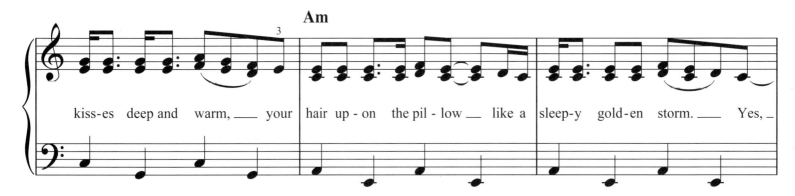

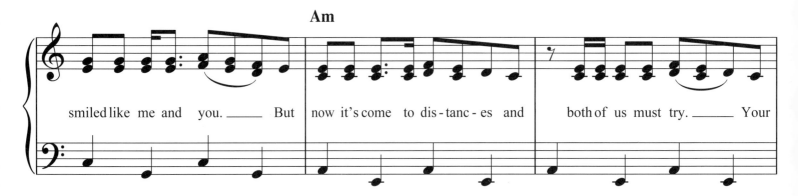

F   **G**

eyes   are soft with sor - row. ___   Hey, that's ___   no   way ___   to say ___   good-

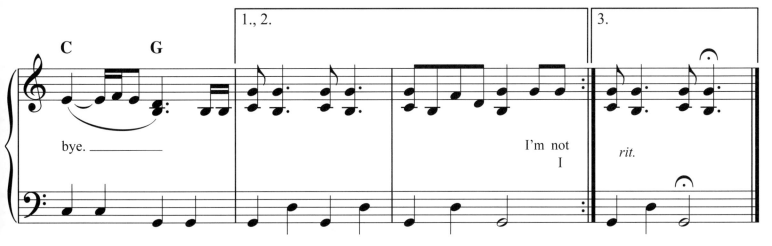

C   **G**   1., 2.   3.

bye. _____   I'm not   *rit.*
                                        I

Additional Lyrics

2. I'm not looking for another
   As I wander in my time
   Walk me to the corner
   Our steps will always rhyme
   You know my love goes with you
   As your love stays with me
   It's just the way it changes
   Like the shoreline and the sea
   But let's not talk of love or chains
   And things we can't untie
   Your eyes are soft with sorrow
   Hey, that's no way to say goodbye

3. I loved you in the morning
   Our kisses deep and warm
   Your hair upon the pillow
   Like a sleepy golden storm
   Yes, many loved before us
   I know that we are not new
   In the city and in forest
   They smiled like me and you
   But let's not talk of love or chains
   And things we can't untie
   Your eyes are soft with sorrow
   Hey, that's no way to say goodbye

I'M YOUR MAN

Words and Music by
LEONARD COHEN

Moderate, mysterious Swing feel

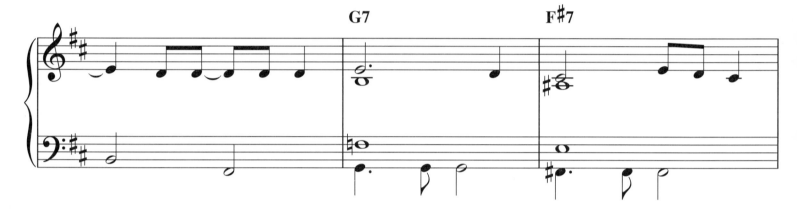

If you want a lov- er, _____ I'll do

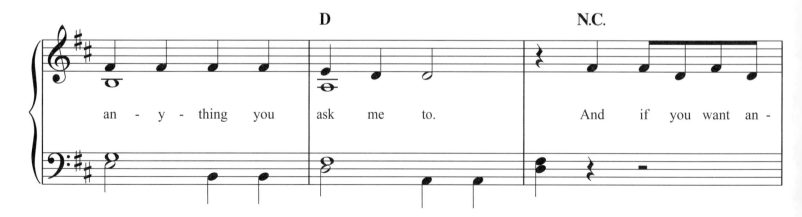

an- y- thing you ask me to. And if you want an-

Em .... **D**

oth - er kind of love, ____ I'll wear a mask for you. ____

N.C. .... **Bm**

If you want a part - ner, take my hand ____ or if you want to

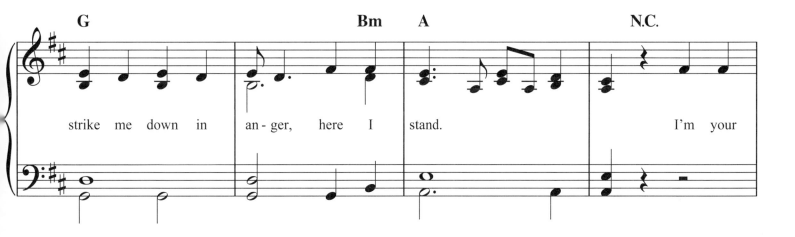

G .... **Bm** **A** .... **N.C.**

strike me down in an - ger, here I stand. I'm your

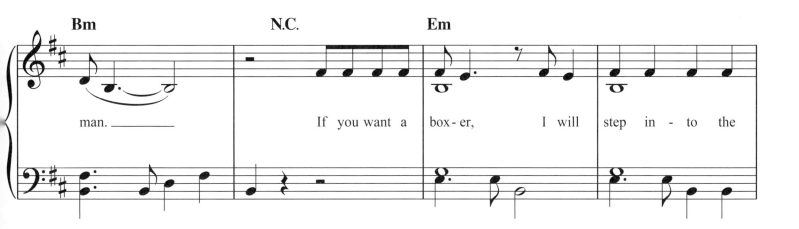

Bm .... **N.C.** .... **Em**

man. _____ If you want a box - er, I will step in - to the

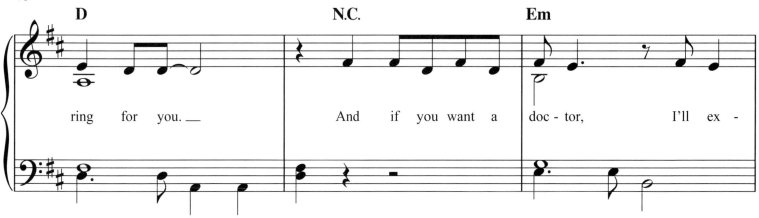

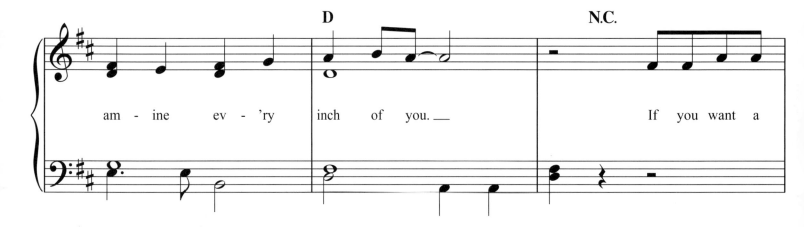

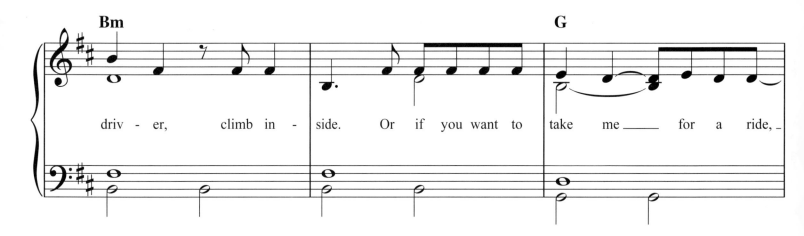

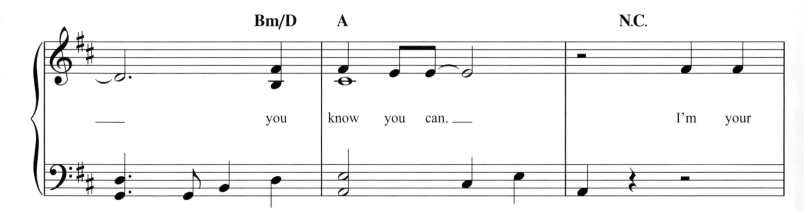

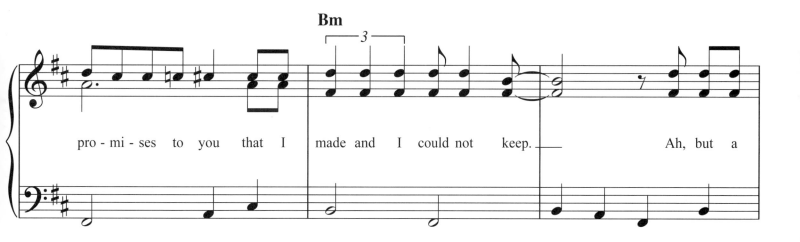

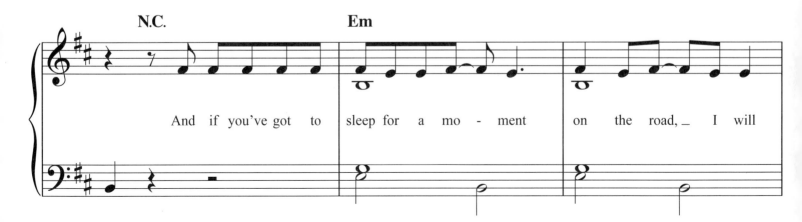

steer for you. ___ And if you want to work the street a - lone ___

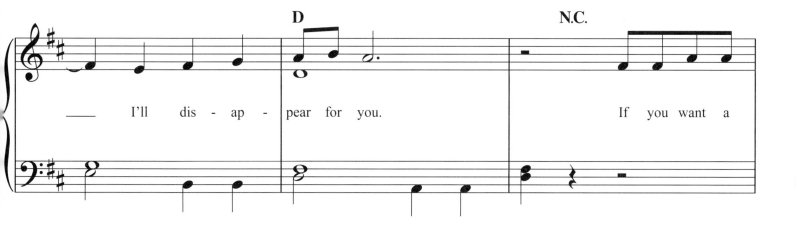

___ I'll dis - ap - pear for you. If you want a

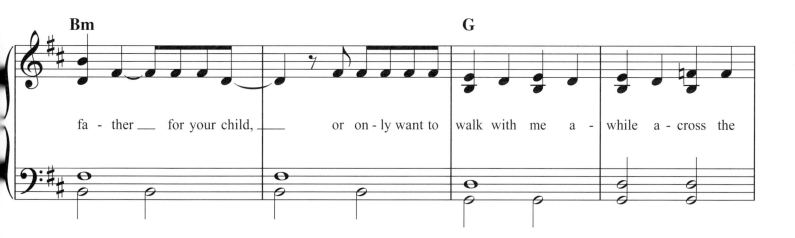

fa - ther ___ for your child, ___ or on - ly want to walk with me a - while a - cross the

Freely

sand, ___ I'm your man. ___
molto rall.

A THOUSAND KISSES DEEP

Words and Music by LEONARD COHEN
and SHARON ROBINSON

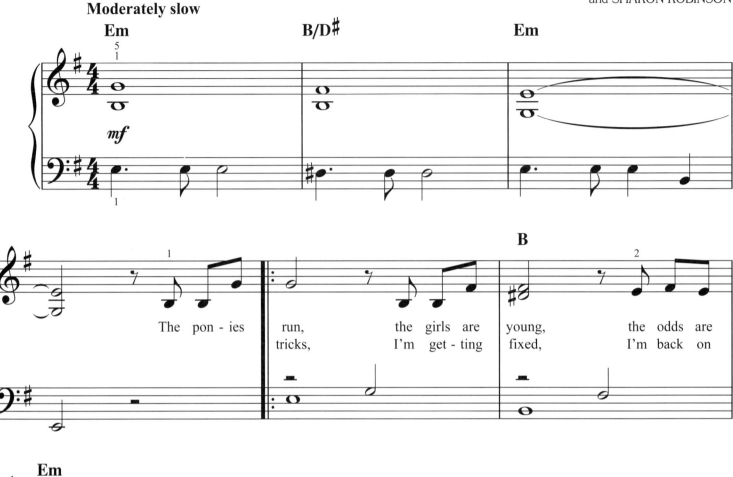

now   to   deal   with your   in - vin - ci - ble de - feat, __
I   had miles   to drive,   and prom - is - es to keep; __

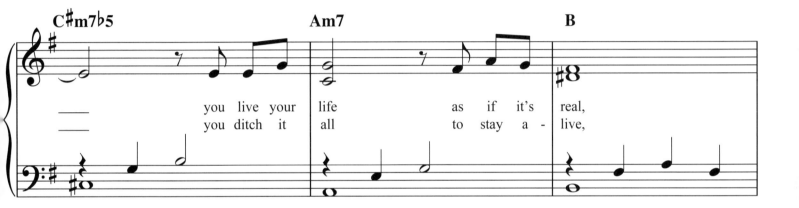

__   you live your life   as if it's real,
__   you ditch it all   to stay a - live,

a thou - sand kis - ses deep. __   I'm run - ning
a thou - sand kis - ses deep. __

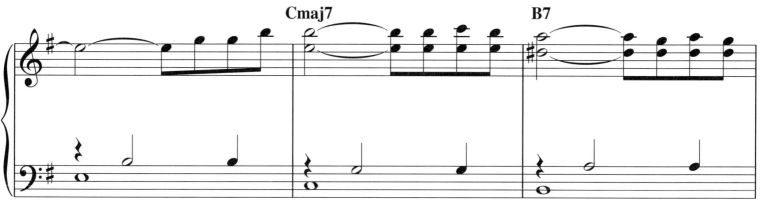

And some-times when the night is

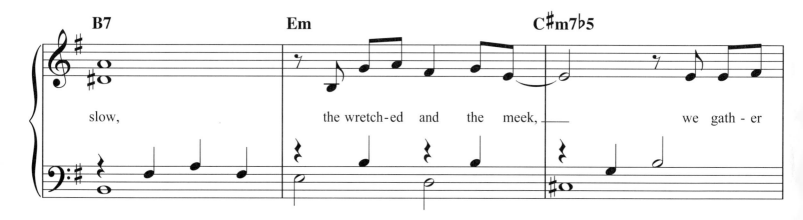

slow, the wretch-ed and the meek, we gath - er

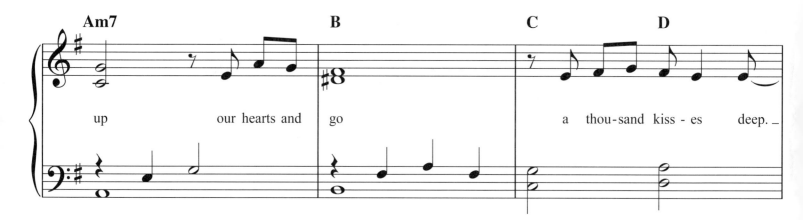

up our hearts and go a thou-sand kiss - es deep.

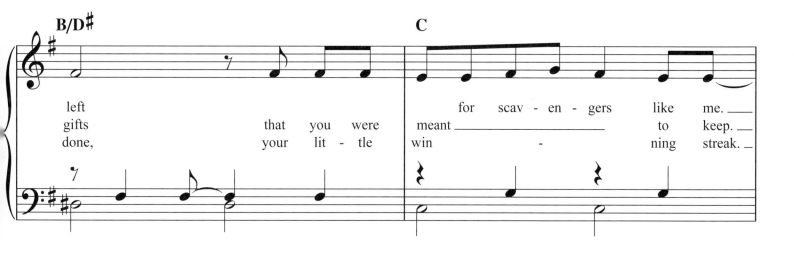

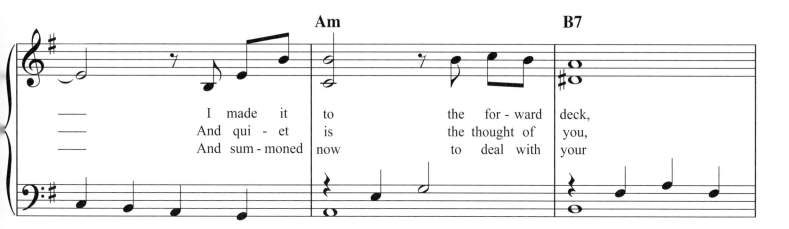

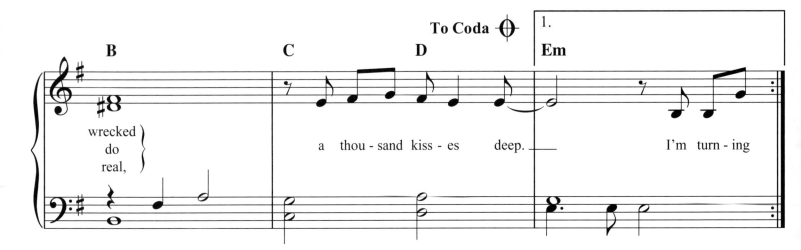

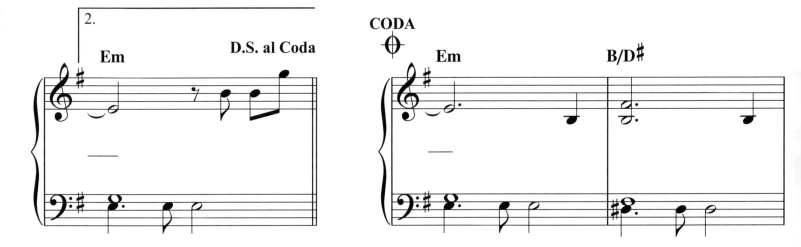

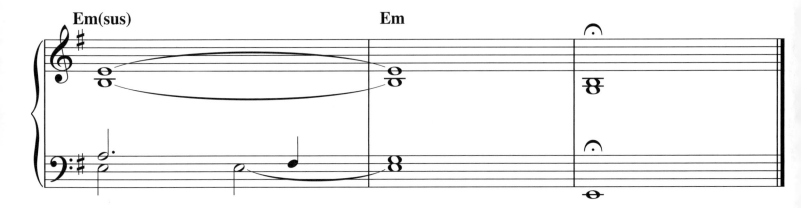

SO LONG MARIANNE

Words and Music by
LEONARD COHEN

Moderately slow, in 2

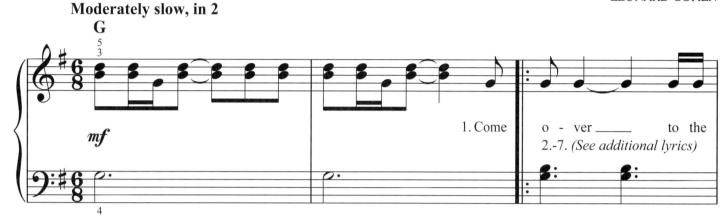

1. Come o - ver ___ to the
2.-7. *(See additional lyrics)*

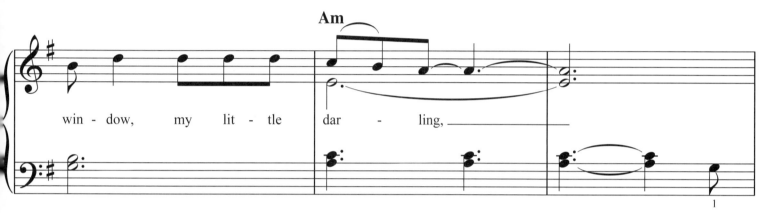

win - dow, my lit - tle dar - ling, ___

I'd like to try to read your palm. ___

___ I used to think I was some ___ sort of

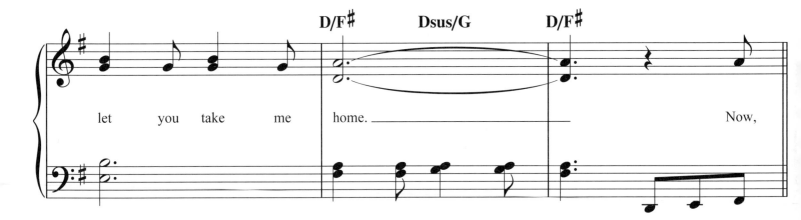

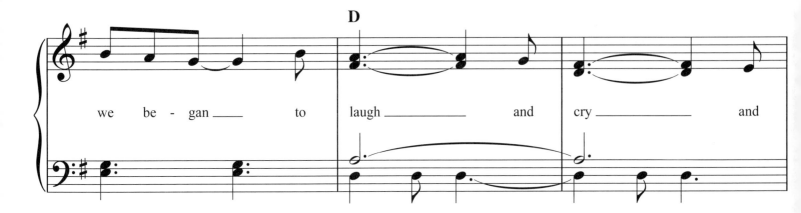

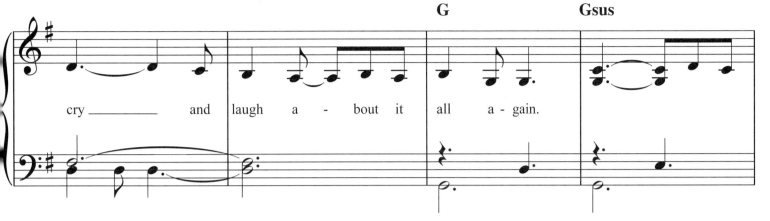

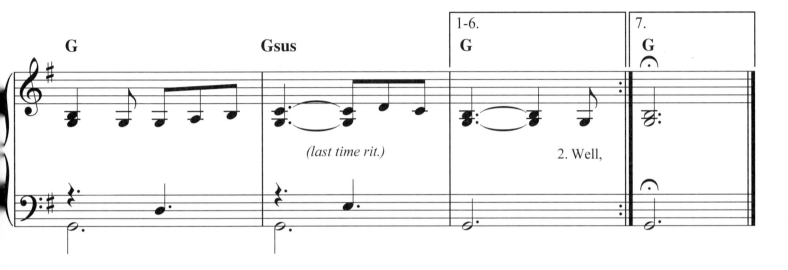

Additional Lyrics

2. Well, you know that I love to live with you
But you make me forget so very much
I forget to pray for the angel
And then the angels forget to pray for us
Chorus

3. We met when we were almost young
Deep in the green lilac park
You held on to me like I was a crucifix
As we went kneeling through the dark
Chorus

4. Your letters, they all say that you're beside me now
Then why do I feel alone?
I'm standing on a ledge, and your fine spider web
Is fastening my ankle to a stone.
Chorus

5. For now I need your hidden love
I'm cold as a new razor blade
You left when I told you I was curious
I never said I was brave
Chorus

6. Oh, you're really such a pretty one
I see you've gone and changed your name again
And just when I climbed this whole mountainside
To wash my eyelids in the rain
Chorus

7. O your eyes, well, I forget your eyes
Your body's at home in every sea
How come you gave away your news to everyone
That you said was a secret for me?
Chorus

SUZANNE

Words and Music by
LEONARD COHEN

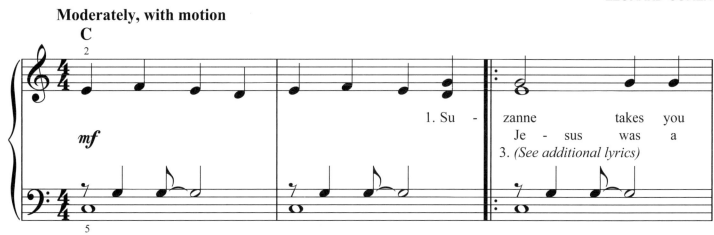

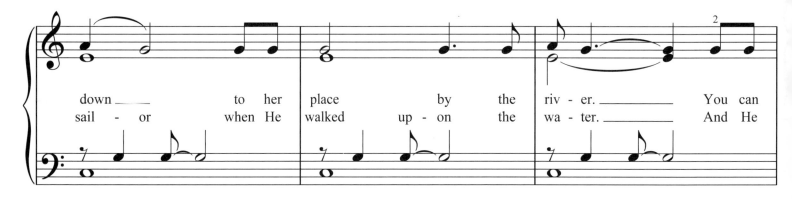

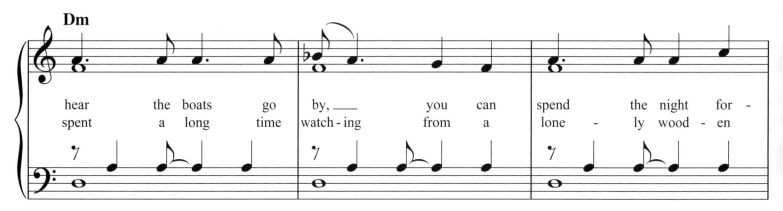

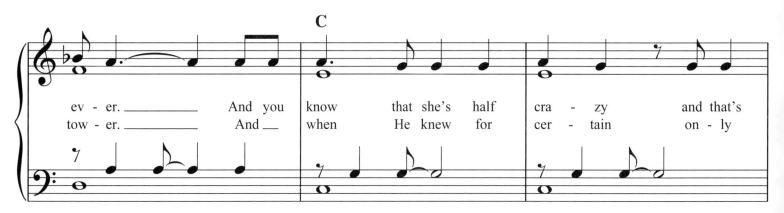

why you want to be there; and she feeds you tea and
drown - ing men could see Him, He said, "All men shall be

o - rang - es that came all the way from Chi - na. And
sail - ors then, un - til the sea shall free them." But

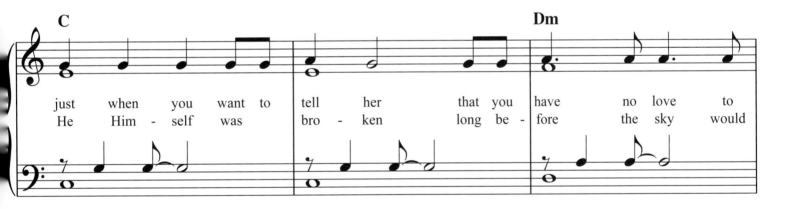

just when you want to tell her that you have no love to
He Him - self was bro - ken long be - fore the sky would

give her, she gets you on her wave - length and
o - pen. For - sak - en, al - most hu - man, He

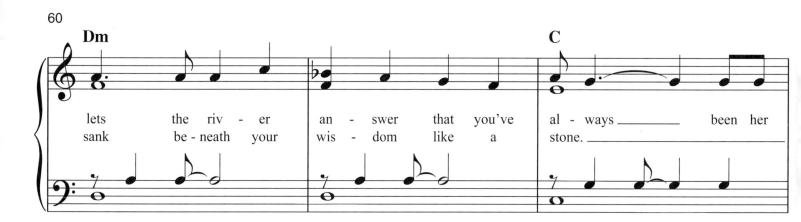

lets   the riv - er   an - swer that you've   al - ways _____ been her
sank   be - neath your   wis - dom like   a   stone. _____

lov - er. _____   And   you
_____   And   you

want   to trav - el   with her, _____ and you want   to trav - el
want   to trav - el   with Him, _____ and you want   to trav - el

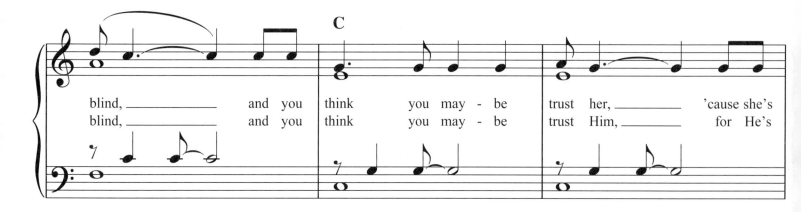

blind, _____ and you think   you may - be   trust her, _____ 'cause she's
blind, _____ and you think   you may - be   trust Him, _____ for He's

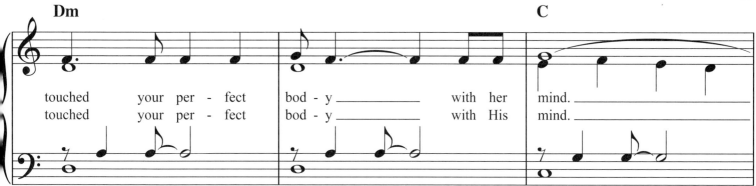

Dm   **C**

touched   your per - fect   bod - y ____ with her   mind. ____

touched   your per - fect   bod - y ____ with His   mind. ____

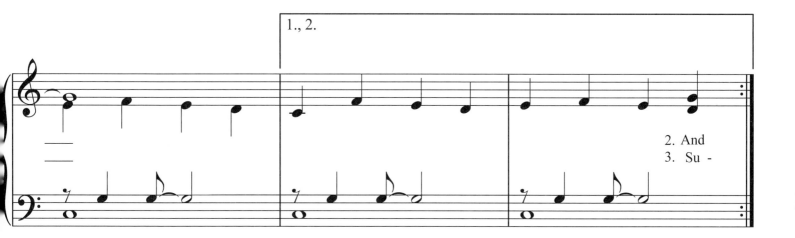

1., 2.

2. And
3. Su -

3.

rit.

Additional Lyrics

3. Suzanne takes you down to her place by the river.
   You can hear the boats go by, you can spend the night forever.
   And the sun pours down like honey on our lady of the harbor;
   And she shows you where to look amid the garbage and the flowers.
   There are heroes in the seaweed. There are children in the morning.
   They are leaning out for love, and they will lean that way forever
   While Suzanne holds her mirror.
   And you want to travel with her,
   And you want to travel blind,
   And you think maybe you'll trust her,
   For you've touched her perfect body with your mind.

WAITING FOR THE MIRACLE

Words and Music by LEONARD COHEN
and SHARON ROBINSON

Slow and steady

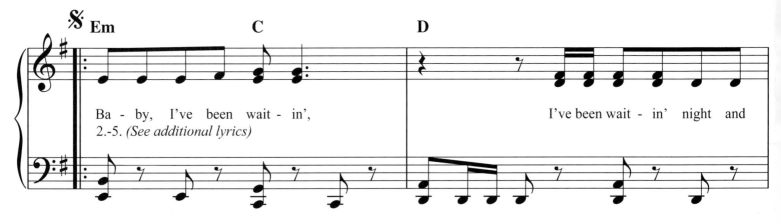

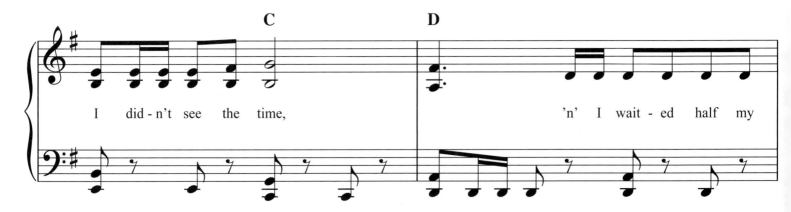

life a - way.   There were

lots of in - vi - ta - tions,   I know you sent me

some.   But I was

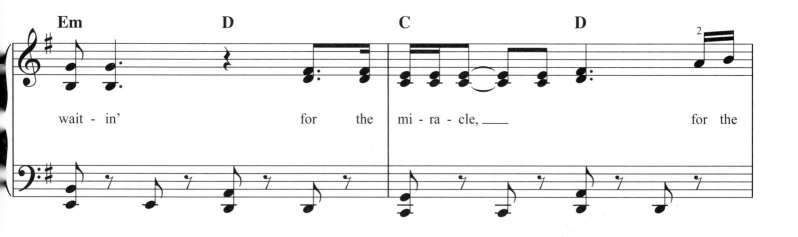

wait - in'   for the   mi - ra - cle, ____   for the

D♯dim   **B7♯5**

mi - ra - cle to come.

Em   **1., 2., 4.**

2. I
3. I
5. Now

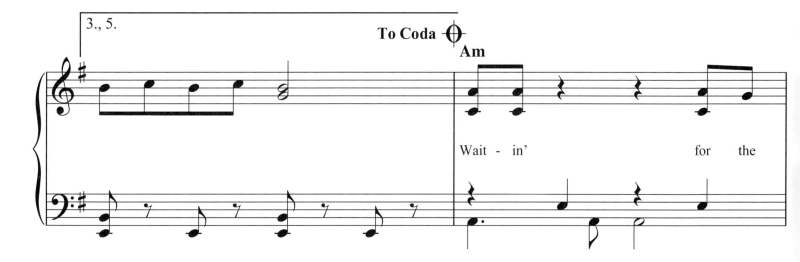

3., 5.   **To Coda**   **Am**

Wait - in'   for the

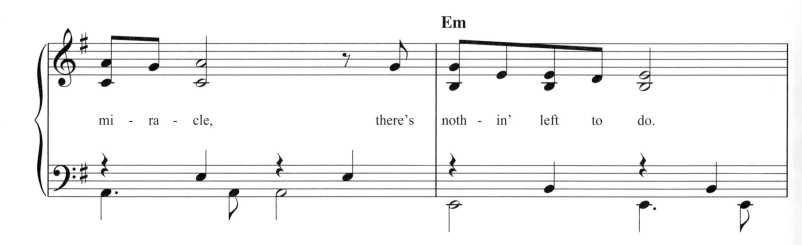

                                             Em

mi - ra - cle,   there's noth - in' left to do.

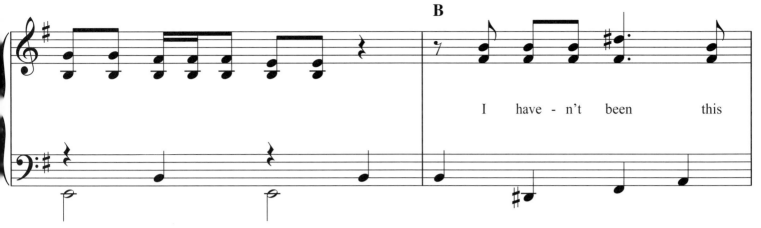

I have-n't been this

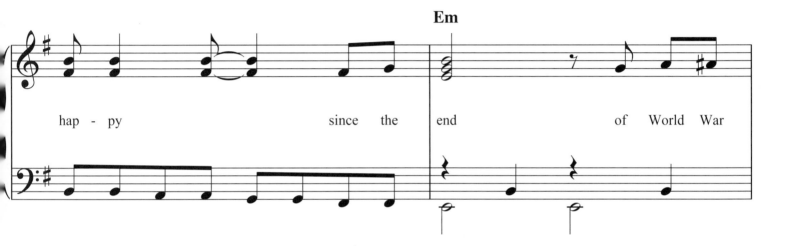

hap - py   since the   end   of World War

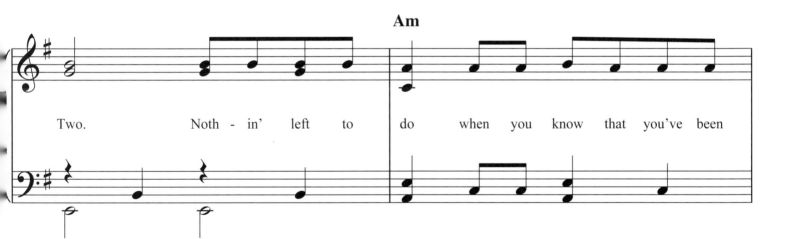

Two.   Noth - in' left to   do   when you know that you've been

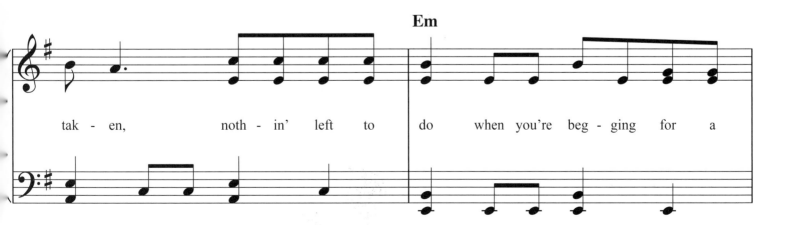

tak - en,   noth - in' left to   do   when you're beg - ging for a

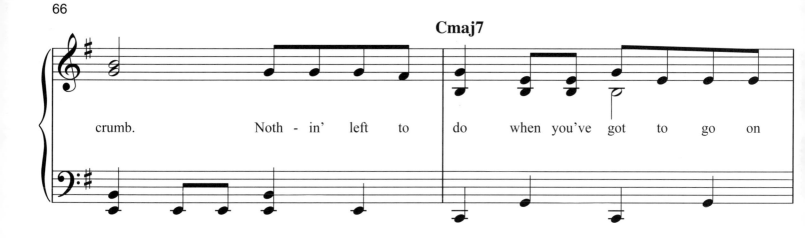

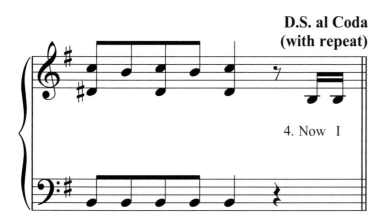

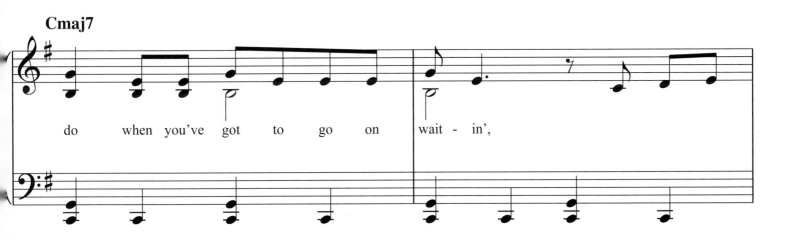

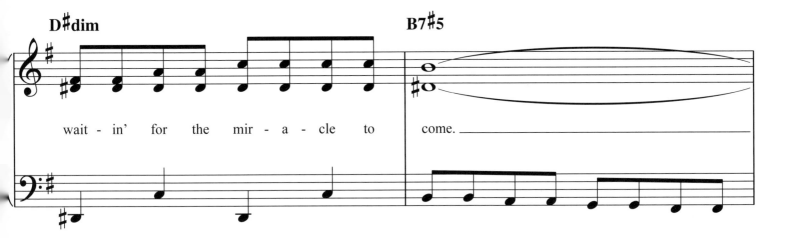

6. When you've

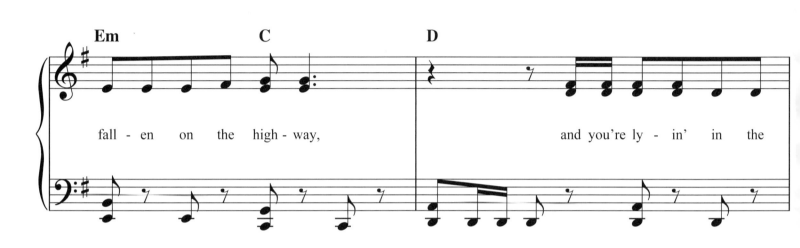

fall - en on the high - way, and you're ly - in' in the

rain, and they

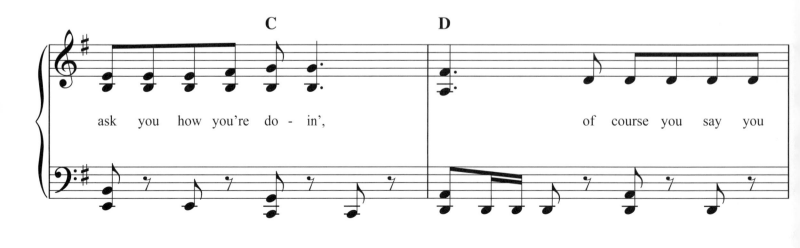

ask you how you're do - in', of course you say you

Em

can't com - plain.   If you're

D

squeezed for   in - for - ma - tion,   that's   when you've got   to   play   it

D♯dim   B+

dumb,   you   just   say   you're   out   there

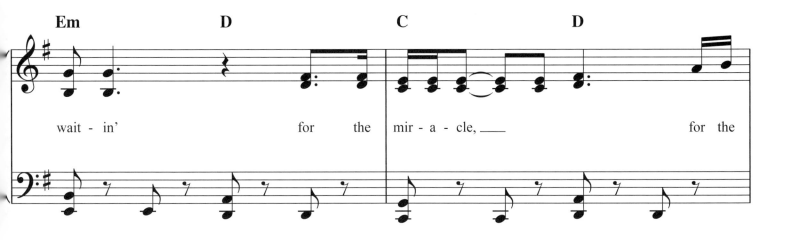

Em   D   C   D

wait - in'   for   the   mir - a - cle, ____   for   the

Additional Lyrics

2. I know you really love me,
   But, you see, my hands were tied.
   And I know it must have hurt you,
   It must have hurt your pride
   To have to stand beneath my window
   With your bugle and your drum.
   And me, I'm up there waitin'
   For the miracle, for the miracle to come.

3. I don't believe you'd like it,
   You wouldn't like it here.
   There ain't no entertainment,
   And the judgements are severe.
   The Maestro says it's Mozart,
   But it sounds like bubble gum.
   When you're waitin'
   For the miracle, for the miracle to come.

4. Now I dreamed about you, baby,
   It was just the other night.
   Most of you was naked,
   Ah, but some of you was light.
   The sands of time were fallin'
   From your fingers and your thumb,
   And you were waitin'
   For the miracle, for the miracle to come.

5. Now baby, let's get married,
   We've been alone too long
   Let's be alone together,
   Let's see if we're that strong.
   Yeah, let's do somethin' crazy
   Somethin' absolutely wrong,
   While we're waitin'
   For the miracle, for the miracle to come.